BANFF

POCKET TRAVEL GUIDE

●••••••••••••••••••••••••••●

Travel smarter, not harder,

with this insider's guide.

John Stone C.

Let the mountains be your teacher, the rivers your guide, and the wilderness your sanctuary...

Disclaimer:

While we have diligently strived for accuracy in this guide, please note that details like prices, hours, and contact information may change. We encourage you to confirm these details with official sources before your trip.

BOOK CONTENTS

INTRODUCTION...12

What Makes This Guide Special   14

CHAPTER 1

WELCOME TO BANFF NATIONAL PARK

- A Jewel in the Canadian Rockies 16
- Why Banff is Special: Nature's Masterpiece   17
- Geography and Landscape: Where Mountains Meet Magic   19
- Fun Facts & Hidden Gems: Discover Banff's Secrets   21

CHAPTER 2: BEFORE YOU GO

- Things You Should Know When Traveling to Banff   24
- Weather Considerations   26
- Visas & Essentials   27
- Money Matters: Managing Your Finances in Banff   28
- Travel Budget Planner: Making the Most of Your Money 29
- Best Time to Travel to Banff   32

CHAPTER 3: GETTING AROUND

- Arriving & Departing 36
- Getting to Banff Townsite 38
- Transportation within Banff and the Surrounding Area   38

CHAPTER 4: BANFF WITH KIDS

- Family-Friendly Attractions 41
- Kid-Approved Activities   43
- Tips for Traveling with Children 44

CHAPTER 5: MUST-SEE SIGHTS

- Iconic Landmarks   45
- Scenic Drives & Viewpoints   47
- Hiking Trails for All Levels 48
- Wildlife Viewing Opportunities   49

CHAPTER 6: OFF-THE-BEATEN-PATH

- Hidden Gems & Local Secrets   50
- Unique Experiences 52

Chapter 7: Local Flavors

- Must-Try Dishes   54
- Cafés & Restaurants 62
- Grocery Stores & Markets 68

CHAPTER 8: BANFF AFTER DARK

- Bars & Pubs   69
- Live Music & Entertainment   70
- Stargazing & Northern Lights   71

CHAPTER 9: DAY TRIPS & EXCURSIONS

- Yoho National Park   73
- Lake Louise Ski Resort   74
- Canmore & Kananaskis Country 76

CHAPTER 10: ACCOMMODATIONS

- Hostels 78
- Campgrounds 80
- Hotels   82

CHAPTER 11

ACTIVITIES & EXPERIENCES

- Summer Adventures: 87
- Winter Activities   90
- Relaxation & Wellness   92
- Festivals & Events   92

CHAPTER 12: PRACTICAL TIPS

- Local Customs & Etiquette 94
- Things to Avoid   96
- Staying Safe & Connected: Emergency Contacts and Communication Tips 99
- Languages Spoken: 100
- Medical Services & Pharmacies   101

CHAPTER 13:

SUGGESTED ITINERARIES

- Suggested Itineraries   103
- Short & Sweet (2-3 Days) 103
- A Week in Banff   105
- Extended Stay (10+ days) 107
- Conclusion   108
- Word Search Fun   110
- Journals 116

HOW TO USE THIS GUIDE:

This Banff travel guide is designed to be your ultimate companion for exploring the wonders of Banff National Park. Some tips on how to make the most of it include:

- **Before You Go:**

  - ✓ Browse the guide to get acquainted with Banff.

  - ✓ Review essential pre-trip info in the "Before You Go" chapter.

  - ✓ Use the Travel Budget Planner.

  - ✓ Choose activities and attractions you're excited about.

  - ✓ Craft your itinerary using our suggestions or personalize it!

- **While You're There:**

  - ✓ Carry the guide with you for easy reference.

  - ✓ Use the maps for navigation.

  - ✓ Check "Practical Tips" for cultural insights and safety info.

  - ✓ Embrace spontaneous adventures and detours!

✓ Most importantly, have fun and enjoy Banff's beauty!

Bonus Tips:

- **Full-Color Photos**

- **Word Search Puzzles**

- **QR Codes:** Scan for additional information and resources.

- Highlight or mark your favorite spots.

- Jot down your own notes and memories.

How to Scan the QR Codes

Throughout this guide, you'll find QR codes that link directly to Google Maps directions for various locations.

1. Launch your camera app and position it over the code.

2. Tap the notification to open the Google Maps directions.

3. Select your starting point (e.g., your current location or your hotel) and tap "Start" to begin navigation.

4. Choose your mode of transportation (walking, driving, etc.).

5. Tap "Start" to begin your journey!

If you don't see a notification, you may need to enable QR code scanning in your camera settings or download a QR code reader app from your app store.

Travel opens your heart, broadens your mind, and fills your life with stories to tell." - Paula Bendfeldt

INTRODUCTION

Years ago, armed with a worn backpack and a spirit of adventure, I began my first solo trip to Banff National Park. The moment I stepped off the bus and gazed upon the majestic mountains, I was utterly captivated. The sheer scale and beauty of the landscape took my breath away, and I knew I had stumbled upon a place that would forever hold a special place in my heart.

As a travel guide writer, I've had the privilege of exploring countless destinations around the world. But Banff, with its pristine wilderness, abundant wildlife, and charming mountain town atmosphere, remains one of my all-time

favorites. I've hiked its rugged trails, paddled its serene lakes, and witnessed the magic of the Northern Lights dancing across its night sky. And with each visit, I discover something new, another layer of wonder that makes this park so extraordinary.

Now, I'm excited to share my passion for Banff with you. This pocket travel guide is more than just a collection of facts and recommendations; it's a distillation of my experiences and insights, designed to help you create your own unforgettable adventure.

Within these pages, you'll find insider tips, hidden gems, and practical advice gleaned from years of exploration. Whether you're a seasoned hiker seeking challenging trails or a first-time visitor eager to experience Banff's iconic landmarks, this guide will be your trusted companion.

I want to encourage you to embrace the spirit of discovery and let Banff's natural beauty inspire you. Push your limits, try new things, and make memories you'll cherish forever. This guide is your starting point, but the true adventure lies in the journey you'll create for yourself.

So, pack your bags, lace up your hiking boots, and get ready to experience the magic of Banff National Park. I can't wait to hear about the incredible adventures you'll have!

What Makes This Guide Special

- **Concise Yet Comprehensive:** We've packed all the essential information you need into a pocket-sized format, so you can easily carry it with you as you explore Banff. No more lugging around a bulky guidebook!

- **Insider Tips & Local Secrets:** Discover hidden gems and off-the-beaten-path experiences that most tourists miss, thanks to our in-depth knowledge of the area.

- **Stunning Visuals:** Full-color photos and detailed maps bring Banff's beauty to life, helping you visualize your adventure and plan your itinerary.

- **Practical Advice for a Smooth Trip:** We've included everything from packing tips and transportation options to wildlife safety and local customs, ensuring you're well-prepared for your journey.

- **Personalized Itineraries:** Choose from suggested itineraries tailored to different interests and timeframes, or create your own adventure using our expert recommendations.

- **Family-Friendly Focus:** We've included a dedicated chapter with tips and suggestions for traveling with kids, ensuring everyone in the family has a memorable experience.

- **Interactive & Engaging:** Word search puzzles add a touch of fun and challenge, while travel journal prompts encourage you to reflect on your experiences and create lasting memories.

- **Easy Booking:** We've provided detailed contact information for all recommended accommodations, making it easy to book your perfect stay.

Whether you're a seasoned adventurer or a first-time visitor, this guide is your key to unlocking the magic of Banff National Park.

CHAPTER 1
WELCOME TO BANFF NATIONAL PARK!

A Jewel in the Canadian Rockies

Nestled in the heart of the Canadian Rockies, Banff National Park is a true gem, a sprawling wilderness that has captivated the hearts of adventurers and nature lovers for generations. Recognized as a UNESCO World Heritage Site, Banff's breathtaking landscapes are a testament to the raw power and beauty of nature.

Spanning over 6,641 square kilometers (2,564 square miles), Banff is a vast playground of towering peaks, ancient glaciers, crystal-clear lakes, and lush forests. It's a place where you can hike to stunning viewpoints, kayak on turquoise waters, spot wildlife in their natural habitat, and simply breathe in the fresh mountain air. Whether you're seeking adrenaline-pumping adventures or peaceful moments of solitude in nature, Banff National Park offers an unforgettable experience for every traveler.

Why Banff is Special: Nature's Masterpiece

Banff National Park stands out as a truly exceptional destination for several reasons:

- **Awe-Inspiring Scenery:** Banff's landscapes are nothing short of breathtaking. Imagine towering snow-capped peaks, shimmering turquoise lakes, cascading waterfalls, and verdant valleys teeming with wildflowers. Every turn reveals a new vista, a postcard-worthy scene that will leave you in awe of nature's artistry.

- **Abundant Wildlife:** Banff is a haven for wildlife, offering a chance to encounter iconic Canadian animals in their natural habitat. Keep your eyes peeled for elk, deer, bighorn sheep, mountain goats, and even bears as you explore the park's trails and scenic drives.

- **Outdoor Adventures Galore:** Whether you're an avid hiker, a seasoned skier, or simply enjoy a leisurely stroll in nature, Banff has something for everyone. Hike to stunning viewpoints, bike along scenic trails, kayak on pristine lakes, or hit the slopes at world-class ski resorts. There's no limit to the outdoor adventures you can have.

- **Charming Town of Banff:** Nestled in the heart of the park, the town of Banff offers a delightful blend of small-town charm and cosmopolitan amenities. Stroll down Banff Avenue, lined with shops, restaurants, and art galleries, or relax in a cozy café with a warm cup of coffee and a view of the mountains.

- **Unforgettable Experiences:** Beyond its natural beauty and outdoor activities, Banff offers a range of unique experiences. Soak in the Banff Upper Hot Springs, marvel at the ice formations in Johnston Canyon during winter, or witness the magic of the Northern Lights dancing across the night sky.

Banff National Park is a place that will stay with you long after you leave. It's a destination that inspires awe, ignites adventure, and leaves you with a profound appreciation for the natural world.

Geography and Landscape: Where Mountains Meet Magic

Banff National Park is nestled in the heart of the Canadian Rockies, a majestic mountain range that stretches across western Canada. Located in the province of Alberta, the park encompasses a vast and varied landscape, shaped by millions of years of geological forces.

Key Features:

- **Mountain Ranges:** Banff is dominated by towering peaks, including Mount Rundle, Cascade Mountain, and Mount Norquay. These rugged giants, formed through tectonic plate collisions and volcanic activity, create a dramatic backdrop for the park's scenic wonders.

- **Glaciers & Icefields:** Remnants of the last ice age, glaciers and icefields like the Columbia Icefield continue to shape the landscape, carving valleys, creating lakes, and feeding rivers with their meltwater.

- **Rivers & Lakes:** The park is crisscrossed by rivers, most notably the Bow River, which winds its way through the valley, providing a lifeline for wildlife and opportunities for recreation. Banff is also home to numerous picturesque lakes, including the iconic Lake Louise and Moraine Lake, known for their vibrant turquoise hues.

- **Forests & Meadows:** Lush forests of pine, spruce, and fir trees blanket the slopes, providing habitat for a variety of wildlife. Wildflower-filled meadows add splashes of color to the landscape, especially during the summer months.

The Impact of Glaciers:

Glaciers have played a crucial role in shaping Banff's dramatic landscape. Over millennia, these massive rivers of ice carved deep valleys, sculpted mountain peaks, and created the stunning lakes that dot the park. Today, remnants of these glaciers can still be seen, reminding us of the powerful forces that have shaped this natural wonderland.

As you explore Banff, you'll witness the remarkable interplay between mountains, glaciers, rivers, and forests, creating a blend of beauty and biodiversity that's truly awe-inspiring.

Fun Facts & Hidden Gems: Discover Banff's Secrets

Beyond the iconic landmarks and popular trails, Banff National Park holds a treasure trove of fascinating stories and hidden wonders just waiting to be discovered.

- **Did You Know?** Banff is Canada's oldest national park, established in 1885 after the discovery of natural hot springs. It was originally named Rocky Mountains Park, but was later renamed Banff in 1930 after Banffshire in Scotland.

- **Wildlife Haven:** Banff is home to over 50 species of mammals, including grizzly bears, black bears, elk, deer, moose, bighorn sheep, mountain goats, wolves, and coyotes. Stay alert! There could be surprises around the corner.

- **Cave and Basin National Historic Site:** Step back in time at the birthplace of Canada's national parks. Explore the natural hot springs that sparked the park's creation and learn about Banff's rich history and geology.

- **Ink Pots:** Venture off the beaten path and hike to the Ink Pots, a cluster of colorful mineral springs bubbling up from the earth. The vibrant hues of blue, green, and orange are a sight to behold.

- **Sundance Canyon:** Escape the crowds at Johnston Canyon and discover the quieter beauty of Sundance Canyon. Hike through a lush forest, marvel at cascading waterfalls, and enjoy a peaceful picnic by the creek.

- **Two Jack Lake:** This picturesque lake, located just a short drive from Banff Townsite, offers stunning views of Mount Rundle and the surrounding peaks. It's a perfect spot for canoeing, kayaking, or simply relaxing on the shore.

- **Vermilion Lakes:** These three interconnected lakes are known for their calm waters and breathtaking reflections of Mount Rundle at sunrise and sunset. Rent a canoe or kayak for a peaceful paddle, or simply enjoy a leisurely stroll along the shoreline.

- **Tunnel Mountain:** For a relatively easy hike with rewarding views, climb to the summit of Tunnel Mountain. The panoramic vista encompasses Banff Townsite, the Bow Valley, and the surrounding mountains.

- **Surprise Corner:** This aptly named viewpoint offers a stunning vista of the Bow River and the Fairmont Banff Springs Hotel. It's a popular spot for photos and a great place to start or end your day of exploration.

These are just a few of the hidden gems and fascinating facts that make Banff National Park so special. As you venture off the beaten path and delve deeper into the park's wonders, you're sure to discover your own unique treasures and create unforgettable memories.

CHAPTER 2: BEFORE YOU GO

Things You Should Know When Traveling to Banff

Before you set off on your Banff journey, there are a few things you should know to ensure a safe and enjoyable trip.

Park Fees & Permits

To help preserve the park's natural beauty and provide essential services, Banff National Park charges entry fees. You'll need a valid park pass displayed on your vehicle's dashboard while driving within the park.

- **Daily Pass:** This option is ideal for short visits and costs around $10 USD per adult and $5 USD per child (ages 6-17). Children under 6 are free.

- **Discovery Pass:** If you plan on visiting multiple national parks in Canada within a year, the Discovery Pass offers unlimited access for a set fee. It's a great value if you're an avid explorer!

Additionally, certain activities within the park may require specific permits. These include:

- **Camping:** You'll need a camping permit to stay overnight in any of the park's campgrounds. t's strongly advised to book in advance, particularly when it's busy.

- **Backcountry Hiking:** If you plan on venturing into the backcountry, you'll need a Wilderness Pass. This helps park officials monitor activity and ensure your safety in remote areas.

Wildlife Safety

Banff is home to a variety of wildlife, including bears, elk, and wolves. While encountering these animals can be thrilling, it's crucial to prioritize safety and respect their natural habitat.

Here are some essential tips:

- **Maintain a safe distance:** Always observe wildlife from a safe distance, at least 100 meters (328 feet) for bears and 30 meters (98 feet) for other large animals.

- **Never feed wildlife:** Feeding wildlife can alter their natural behavior and create dangerous situations for both humans and animals.

- **Carry bear spray:** If you're hiking or camping in bear country, carry bear spray and know how to use it properly. It's a highly effective deterrent in case of a close encounter.

- **Store food properly:** When camping, store all food, toiletries, and other scented items in bear-proof containers or lockers provided at campgrounds.

Weather Considerations

Don't be surprised by unexpected weather changes in Banff, even in summer. Mountain weather can change quickly, so be prepared for everything from sunshine and warm temperatures to rain, snow, or even hail.

- **Dress in layers:** Wear clothes that you can easily add or remove as the temperature changes.

- **Bring waterproof gear:** A rain jacket and waterproof hiking boots are essential, even if the forecast looks sunny.

- **Check the forecast:** Before heading out for any outdoor activities, check the latest weather forecast and trail conditions.

By following these tips and being prepared, you can ensure a safe and enjoyable experience in Banff National Park, no matter the season.

Visas & Essentials

Before you pack your bags, let's make sure you have all the necessary travel documents and essentials for a smooth trip to Banff.

Visa Requirements

Canada welcomes visitors from around the world, and many travelers don't need a visa for stays up to six months. However, it's crucial to double-check the specific visa requirements for your country of origin. You can do this by visiting the official Government of Canada website or consulting your nearest Canadian embassy or consulate.

If you do require a visa, you'll typically need to apply well in advance and provide supporting documents like a valid passport, proof of funds, and a detailed itinerary.

Electronic Travel Authorization (eTA)

Even if you don't need a visa, citizens of certain visa-exempt countries flying to or transiting through Canada will need an Electronic Travel Authorization (eTA). You can apply for an eTA online through the Government of Canada website; it's a quick and easy process.

Travel Insurance

While not mandatory, purchasing travel insurance before your trip is highly recommended. This will provide financial protection in case of unforeseen events like trip cancellations, medical emergencies, or lost luggage. It's a little price to pay for peace of mind.

Vaccinations and Health Precautions

No specific vaccinations are required for entry into Canada. However, ensure your routine vaccinations are up-to-date. If you plan on hiking or spending time outdoors, consider packing insect repellent and sunscreen.

Money Matters: Managing Your Finances in Banff

Understanding the local currency and payment options will help you navigate your expenses in Banff.

Currency Exchange

The official currency of Canada is the Canadian dollar, denoted by the symbol CAD. You have a few options for exchanging your currency:

- **ATMs:** The most convenient way to access Canadian dollars is through ATMs, widely available in Banff

Townsite and other populated areas. Keep in mind that your bank may charge foreign transaction fees, so check with them beforehand.

- **Currency Exchange Bureaus:** You'll find these at the Calgary International Airport and in Banff, but they typically have higher fees than ATMs.

- **Banks:** Most banks offer currency exchange services, but their hours might be limited.

Credit Cards & Mobile Payments

Major credit cards like Visa, Mastercard, and American Express are widely accepted in Banff. You can use them for most purchases, including accommodations, restaurants, and activities.

Mobile payment options like Apple Pay and Google Pay are also becoming increasingly common, particularly in larger establishments. However, it's always a good idea to carry some cash, especially for smaller shops, markets, or tipping.

Travel Budget Planner: Making the Most of Your Money

Banff offers experiences for every budget, but it's helpful to have an idea of potential costs before you arrive.

- **Accommodation:**

  - ✓ Budget (hostels, campgrounds): $20-60 USD per night

  - ✓ Mid-Range (hotels, lodges): $100-250 USD per night

  - ✓ Luxury (resorts, chalets): $300+ USD per night

- **Meals:**

  - ✓ Budget (grocery stores, picnics): $15-25 USD per day

  - ✓ Mid-Range (casual dining): $30-50 USD per day

  - ✓ Luxury (fine dining): $75+ USD per day

- **Transportation:**

  - ✓ Park Pass: $10 USD per adult per day

  - ✓ Roam Transit (local bus): $2-6 USD per ride or day pass

  - ✓ Shuttle to Lake Louise: $10-20 USD round trip

  - ✓ Activities: Costs vary depending on the activity. Budget at least $50-100 USD per day for popular activities like gondola rides, boat cruises, or wildlife tours.

Budget-Friendly Tips:

- **Free Activities:** Enjoy the stunning scenery with hikes, walks, and picnics in the park. Visit the Banff Park Museum or Cave and Basin National Historic Site, which offer free admission on certain days.

- **Affordable Dining:** Look for happy hour specials at local pubs or opt for casual eateries and food trucks. Consider packing your own lunches for hikes or day trips.

- **Accommodation Deals:** Travel during the shoulder seasons (spring or fall) for lower accommodation rates. Consider staying outside of Banff Townsite in nearby Canmore for more budget-friendly options.

- **Public Transportation:** Utilize Roam Transit or walk/bike whenever possible to save on transportation costs.

By planning and budgeting wisely, you can experience the wonders of Banff without breaking the bank!

Best Time to Travel to Banff

Banff's beauty transforms with each passing season, offering unique experiences throughout the year. Here's a preview of what you can anticipate:

Summer (June-August)

- **Appeal:** Warm temperatures, long daylight hours, and blooming wildflowers make summer the most popular time to visit.

- **Activities:** Hiking, biking, camping, kayaking, canoeing, horseback riding, wildlife viewing, scenic drives, and gondola rides.

- **Weather:** Days are generally warm and sunny, with average temperatures ranging from 15-25°C (59-77°F). Evenings can be cool, and rain showers are possible.

- **What to Pack**

  ✓ Light layers (t-shirts, shorts, hiking pants)

  ✓ Pack a cozy sweater or fleece jacket in case it gets cool in the evenings.

  ✓ Rain jacket or poncho

  ✓ Sturdy shoes or hiking boots.

- ✓ Sunscreen and sunglasses

- ✓ Insect repellent

- ✓ Swimsuit (for hot springs or lakes)

Fall (September-October)

- **Appeal:** Vibrant fall foliage, crisp air, and fewer crowds create a magical atmosphere.

- **Activities:** Hiking, scenic drives, wildlife viewing, horseback riding, photography.

- **Weather:** Temperatures cool down, ranging from 5-15°C (41-59°F). Expect some rain and the possibility of early snowfall at higher elevations.

- **What to Pack:**

- ✓ Warm layers (long-sleeved shirts, sweaters, fleece jacket)

- ✓ Waterproof jacket and pants

- ✓ Hiking boots or sturdy walking shoes

- ✓ Hat and gloves

Winter (November-March)

- **Appeal:** A winter wonderland of snow-covered peaks, frozen lakes, and festive activities.

- **Activities:** Skiing, snowboarding, snowshoeing, ice skating, dog sledding, visiting the Ice Hotel.

- **Weather:** Cold and snowy, with temperatures often below freezing. Expect an average of -10 to -20°C (14 to -4°F).

- **What to Pack:**

> ✓ Warm base layers (thermal underwear, long johns)
>
> ✓ Insulated mid-layers (fleece jacket, wool sweater)
>
> ✓ Waterproof and insulated winter coat and pants
>
> ✓ Warm hat, scarf, and gloves or mittens
>
> ✓ Waterproof winter boots with good traction

Spring (April-May)

- **Appeal:** Melting snow reveals vibrant wildflowers and wildlife emerges from hibernation.

- **Activities:** Hiking, biking, wildlife viewing, enjoying the quieter atmosphere of the park.

- **Weather:** Temperatures gradually warm up, ranging from 0-15°C (32-59°F). Expect some rain and lingering snow at higher elevations.

- **What to Pack:**

> ✓ Layers (t-shirts, long-sleeved shirts, sweaters, light jacket)
>
> ✓ Waterproof jacket and pants
>
> ✓ Hiking boots or sturdy walking shoes
>
> ✓ Hat and gloves

Key Packing Tip:

Regardless of the season, **layering is key** in Banff. Temperatures can fluctuate throughout the day, especially at higher elevations. Pack versatile clothing items that you can easily add or remove as needed. And don't forget to prioritize comfort and functionality when choosing your footwear!

With this packing guide, you'll be well-prepared to enjoy Banff's beauty in any season!

CHAPTER 3: GETTING AROUND

Arriving & Departing

Most visitors to Banff National Park begin their journey at Calgary International Airport (YYC), the closest major airport, located about 1.5 hours from Banff townsite. From there, you have a few options to reach your mountain paradise:

- **Airport Shuttles:** Several convenient shuttle services operate between the airport and Banff, offering comfortable transportation with multiple daily departures. The cost is typically around $60-70 USD per person, one-way.

- **Driving:** If you prefer the freedom and flexibility of having your own vehicle, renting a car at the airport is a great option. Banff is easily accessible via the Trans-Canada Highway, a scenic route that winds through the breathtaking mountain scenery. However, be aware that parking can be limited and expensive in Banff Townsite, especially during peak season. Also, winter driving conditions can be challenging, so ensure you're prepared with winter tires and have experience driving in snowy or icy conditions.

- **Other Options:** For those seeking alternative transportation, consider the Banff Airporter bus service or the scenic Rocky Mountaineer train journey. These options may require additional planning and booking, but they offer a unique and memorable travel experience. You can find more information and schedules on their respective websites.

Getting to Banff Townsite

Once you've arrived in the Banff area, here's how to reach the charming townsite:

- **Airport Shuttles:** As mentioned earlier, airport shuttles are a convenient and hassle-free way to reach Banff Townsite directly from the airport. They offer door-to-door service, dropping you off at your hotel or accommodation.

- **Rental Cars:** If you've opted for a rental car, simply follow the signs for Banff on the Trans-Canada Highway. The drive is straightforward, and you'll be rewarded with stunning mountain views along the way.

Remember, once you're in Banff Townsite, you'll find it's a very walkable and pedestrian-friendly community, so leave the car parked and explore on foot whenever possible.

Transportation within Banff and the Surrounding Area

Getting around Banff and its surrounding areas is easy and convenient, with several transportation options available to suit your needs.

Roam Transit

Roam Transit is Banff's public bus system, offering an affordable and eco-friendly way to explore the park's highlights. Several routes connect Banff Townsite to popular destinations like Lake Louise, Johnston Canyon, the Banff Gondola, and the Banff Upper Hot Springs.

- **Tickets & Passes:** You can purchase single tickets or day passes directly from the bus driver (exact change required). If you plan on using the bus frequently, consider purchasing a multi-day pass for unlimited travel.

- **Schedules & Routes:** Check the Roam Transit website or app for detailed schedules and route information. Buses generally run frequently during peak season, but be mindful of reduced service during off-peak times.

Taxis

Taxis are readily available in Banff Townsite, offering a convenient option for getting around, especially if you have luggage or are traveling with a group. However, keep in mind that taxis can be expensive, so consider using Roam Transit or other options whenever possible.

Free Shuttles

Some hotels and tour operators offer complimentary shuttle services to specific attractions or ski resorts. Check with your accommodation or tour provider to see if they offer this service, as it can be a great way to save on transportation costs.

Walking & Biking

Banff Townsite is incredibly walkable, with many attractions, shops, and restaurants within easy reach. Lace up your comfortable shoes and explore the charming streets, taking in the mountain views and fresh air.

If you prefer to pedal your way around, consider renting a bike. Banff has a well-maintained network of bike paths, including the scenic Banff Legacy Trail, perfect for leisurely rides or more challenging adventures.

By combining these transportation options, you'll have the freedom to explore Banff at your own pace and discover its hidden gems. Remember, sometimes the journey itself is part of the adventure!

CHAPTER 4: BANFF WITH KIDS

Banff National Park isn't just for grown-up adventurers – it's a fantastic destination for families, too! With a mix of kid-friendly attractions, exciting activities, and stunning natural beauty, Banff offers the perfect backdrop for creating unforgettable family memories.

Family-Friendly Attractions

- **Banff Gondola:** Take a thrilling ride up Sulphur Mountain in a fully enclosed gondola, soaring above the treetops to reach the summit. At the top, kids will love exploring the interpretive center, learning about the mountain's ecosystem, and taking a stroll along the boardwalk for breathtaking panoramic views.

- **Cave and Basin National Historic Site:** Step back in time at the birthplace of Canada's national parks. This natural hot spring played a pivotal role in Banff's history, and today it offers interactive exhibits, interpretive trails, and even a chance to see endangered Banff Springs snails!

- **Banff Park Museum:** Spark your kids' curiosity at this engaging museum, where they can learn about Banff's natural and cultural history. Discover fascinating exhibits on local wildlife, Indigenous cultures, and the park's geological wonders.

- **Lake Minnewanka Boat Cruise:** Take a scenic boat tour on Lake Minnewanka, the biggest lake in Banff. Keep your eyes peeled for wildlife sightings like bighorn sheep, eagles, and maybe even a bear! The breathtaking views of the surrounding mountains and the fresh mountain air will create a memorable experience for the whole family.

Kid-Approved Activities

- **Hiking:** Hit the trails and explore Banff's natural beauty. Choose from a variety of family-friendly hikes like Johnston Canyon, with its accessible boardwalk and cascading waterfalls, or the Fenland Trail, a gentle loop through a picturesque marshland teeming with wildlife.

- **Biking:** Rent bikes and pedal along the Banff Legacy Trail, a paved pathway that winds through the Bow Valley, offering stunning views of the mountains and the Bow River. It's a great way to explore the park at a leisurely pace and enjoy quality family time.

- **Canoeing or Kayaking:** Spend a serene afternoon paddling on the crystal-clear waters of Lake Louise or Moraine Lake. Rentals are readily available, and you can even opt for a guided tour for a more informative experience.

- **Swimming:** On hot summer days, cool off at the Banff Recreation Grounds, which features an indoor pool with a fun waterslide. It's a perfect place for kids to splash around and have some active fun.

Tips for Traveling with Children

- **Pack Smart:** Bring layers for unpredictable mountain weather, comfortable shoes for exploring, and plenty of snacks and entertainment for travel time and downtime.

- **Plan a Mix of Activities:** Balance outdoor adventures with indoor options like museums, art galleries, or the Banff Recreation Grounds to cater to everyone's interests and energy levels.

- **Choose Family-Friendly Accommodations:** Look for hotels or vacation rentals with amenities like pools, playgrounds, or kids' clubs to keep the little ones entertained.

- **Be Prepared for Transportation:** If you're using public transportation or hiking with young children, consider bringing a stroller or carrier.

With a little planning and flexibility, traveling to Banff with kids can be a rewarding and unforgettable experience. By incorporating these kid-approved activities and tips into your itinerary, you'll create lasting memories and foster a love for nature and adventure in your children.

CHAPTER 5: MUST-SEE SIGHTS

Prepare to be awestruck by Banff's iconic landmarks and breathtaking scenery. These are the must-see sights that will leave you speechless:

Iconic Landmarks

- **Lake Louise:** A picture-perfect scene awaits at Lake

Louise, where turquoise waters mirror the surrounding snow-capped peaks. Rent a canoe for a leisurely paddle, hike to the Lake Agnes Tea House for stunning views, or simply relax on the lakeshore and soak up the tranquility. The majestic Fairmont Chateau Lake Louise, perched on the edge of the lake, adds to the fairytale ambiance.

- **Moraine Lake:** This glacier-fed lake, nestled in the Valley of the Ten Peaks, boasts a vibrant blue hue that's truly mesmerizing. Arrive early in the morning to beat the crowds and witness the sunrise painting the peaks with golden light. It's a photographer's dream and a moment you'll never forget.

- **Banff Gondola:** Take a thrilling ride to the summit of Sulphur Mountain in a fully enclosed gondola. At the top, you'll be rewarded with panoramic views of the Bow Valley, Banff Townsite, and the surrounding peaks. Explore the interpretive center to learn about the mountain's ecosystem or take a leisurely stroll along the boardwalk.

- **Banff Upper Hot Springs:** Unwind and soak in the soothing waters of these natural hot springs, nestled amidst the mountains. The steam rising from the pools creates a magical atmosphere, and the views are simply breathtaking. Remember to bring your own towel and swimsuit!

- **Johnston Canyon:** Lace up your hiking boots and explore the wonders of Johnston Canyon. This popular trail winds its way through a narrow canyon, showcasing cascading waterfalls, limestone cliffs, and unique geological formations. It's an easy hike suitable for all ages, with several viewpoints along the way.

Scenic Drives & Viewpoints

- **Icefields Parkway:** Begin a scenic drive along the Icefields Parkway, often hailed as one of the most beautiful roads in the world. This 232-kilometer (144-mile) highway connects Banff and Jasper National Parks, offering breathtaking views of glaciers, waterfalls, and turquoise lakes. Must-see stops include Peyto Lake, Bow Lake, and the Columbia Icefield.

- **Bow Valley Parkway:** For a more leisurely drive, take the scenic Bow Valley Parkway, an alternative route to Lake Louise. This road winds its way through the valley, offering ample opportunities for wildlife viewing and stops at picturesque spots like Johnston Canyon and Castle Mountain.

- **Vermilion Lakes:** These three interconnected lakes, just outside of Banff Townsite, are a photographer's paradise. Visit at sunrise or sunset to capture stunning reflections of Mount Rundle and the surrounding peaks in the calm waters.

- **Surprise Corner:** This aptly named viewpoint offers a breathtaking vista of the Bow River and the Fairmont Banff Springs Hotel. It's a perfect spot for photos and a great way to appreciate the grandeur of Banff's landscape.

Hiking Trails for All Levels

- **Easy:** Johnston Canyon, Tunnel Mountain, Fenland Trail

- **Moderate:** Lake Agnes Trail, Sulphur Mountain (without the gondola), Sunshine Meadows

- **Challenging:** Plain of the Six Glaciers Trail, Larch Valley & Sentinel Pass, Devil's Thumb

Wildlife Viewing Opportunities

- **Commonly Seen Animals:** Elk, deer, bighorn sheep, mountain goats, marmots

- **Best Times for Viewing:** Early morning and dusk

- **Safety Tips:** Maintain a safe distance from wildlife, never feed them, and be aware of your surroundings. Carry bear spray and know how to use it properly if you're venturing into bear country.

These are just a few highlights of Banff's incredible natural wonders. With its diverse landscapes and abundant wildlife, every day in Banff is an opportunity for adventure and discovery. So lace up your boots, grab your camera, and get ready to explore!

CHAPTER 6: OFF-THE-BEATEN-PATH

Beyond the postcard-perfect vistas of Lake Louise and Moraine Lake, Banff National Park holds a treasure trove of lesser-known gems and local secrets, just waiting to be discovered.

Hidden Gems & Local Secrets

- **Ink Pots:** Lace up your hiking boots and embark on a scenic trail that leads to the enchanting Ink Pots. These natural mineral springs, nestled in a lush meadow, bubble up from the earth in vibrant shades of blue, green, and orange. It's a unique and otherworldly sight that's well worth the hike.

- **Sundance Canyon:** If you're looking for a quieter alternative to the popular Johnston Canyon, head to Sundance Canyon. This hidden gem offers similar beauty, with cascading waterfalls, towering limestone cliffs, and peaceful hiking trails. It's the perfect escape for those seeking solitude and a deeper connection with nature.

- **Two Jack Lake:** Nestled amidst the mountains, Two Jack Lake is a picturesque oasis that's less crowded than its famous neighbor, Lake Louise. Rent a canoe or kayak and glide across the calm waters, enjoying stunning views of Mount Rundle and the surrounding peaks. Or, simply spread out a blanket on the shore and enjoy a peaceful picnic surrounded by natural beauty.

- **Banff Park Museum:** Step back in time and discover the fascinating stories of Banff's natural and cultural history at the Banff Park Museum. This hidden gem houses exhibits on local wildlife, Indigenous cultures, and the park's geological wonders. It's a great place to learn more about the area and gain a deeper appreciation for its unique heritage.

- **Cave and Basin National Historic Site:** This historic site marks the birthplace of Canada's national parks. Explore the natural hot springs that sparked Banff's creation, wander through the interpretive trails, and marvel at the unique cave formations. The interactive exhibits offer a fascinating glimpse into the park's history and geological significance.

Unique Experiences

- **Horseback Riding:** Saddle up and explore Banff's scenic trails on horseback, just like the early explorers and settlers. Several outfitters offer guided trail rides for all levels, allowing you to experience the park's beauty from a unique perspective.

- **Whitewater Rafting:** Get your adrenaline pumping with a thrilling whitewater rafting adventure on the

Bow River. Experienced guides will lead you through exhilarating rapids and calm stretches, offering a unique blend of excitement and natural beauty.

- **Wildlife Photography Tour:** Capture stunning images of Banff's iconic wildlife with the guidance of a professional photographer. These tours take you to prime viewing spots and provide expert tips on capturing the perfect shot.

- **Helicopter Tour:** Soar above the mountains and lakes of Banff National Park on a scenic helicopter tour. You'll be treated to breathtaking aerial views of glaciers, waterfalls, and hidden valleys, creating memories that will last a lifetime.

These off-the-beaten-path adventures and unique experiences will add an extra layer of depth and excitement to your Banff exploration. So venture beyond the familiar and create your own unforgettable journey through this stunning wilderness.

CHAPTER 7: LOCAL FLAVORS

Banff's culinary scene is a delightful mix of hearty Canadian classics, international flavors, and innovative creations. Here are some must-try dishes and dining experiences to satisfy your cravings:

Must-Try Dishes

1. **Poutine:** This iconic Canadian dish features crispy fries topped with cheese curds and smothered in rich gravy. It's a comfort food staple that's perfect after a day of outdoor adventures.

❖ Where to try it:

a) **The Maple Leaf:** This casual eatery on Banff Avenue is a local favorite for its classic poutine and friendly atmosphere.

Phone: +1 403-762-1888

b) **BeaverTails:** Though known for their sweet pastries, BeaverTails also offers a delicious poutine topped with their signature cinnamon-sugar pastry crumble.

Phone: +1 403-985-0086 or +1 403-985-1977

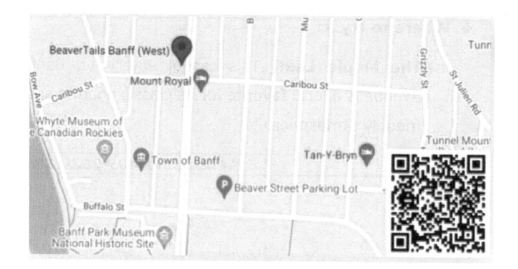

c) **Park Distillery Restaurant + Bar:** For a more upscale take on poutine, try the Park Distillery's Elk Poutine, featuring tender elk meat and wild mushroom gravy.

Phone: +1 403-762-5114

2. **Alberta Beef:** Alberta is renowned for its high-quality beef, and Banff is the perfect place to savor a juicy steak or hearty burger made from locally sourced meat.

❖ **Where to try it:**

a) **The Keg Steakhouse + Bar:** This popular chain offers a classic steakhouse experience with a variety of cuts and preparations.

> *Address: 117 Banff Ave, Banff, AB T1L 1A4, Canada.*
> *Phone: +1 403-760-3030*

b) **Chuck's Steakhouse:** This family-friendly restaurant serves up generous portions of Alberta beef in a casual setting.

> **Address:101 Banff Ave, Banff, AB T1L 1B3, Canada.**
> **Phone number is +1 403-762-4825.**

c) **The Bison Restaurant:** For a unique twist, try the bison burger or steak at this restaurant, which specializes in locally sourced game meats.

> **211 Bear St # 213, Banff, AB T1L 1E4, Canada. Phone is**
> **+1 403-762-5550**

3. **Bannock:** This traditional Indigenous bread is a versatile and delicious staple, often served with savory toppings or enjoyed on its own.

❖ **Where to try it:**

a) **The Buffalo Nations Luxton Museum:** This museum and cultural center in Banff offers a taste of Indigenous cuisine, including bannock.

> **Address: 1 Birch Ave, Banff, AB T1L 1A1, Canada**
> **Phone: +1 403-762-2388**

b) **The Grizzly House:** This unique restaurant serves bannock as part of its fondue experience, allowing you to dip the bread into melted cheese or chocolate.

4. **Maple Syrup Treats:** Canada is synonymous with maple syrup, and you'll find a variety of sweet treats in Banff that showcase this liquid gold.

❖ **Where to try them:**

a) **BeaverTails:** This popular chain is famous for its namesake pastries, which are hand-stretched and topped with various sweet and savory options, including classic cinnamon-sugar and maple butter.

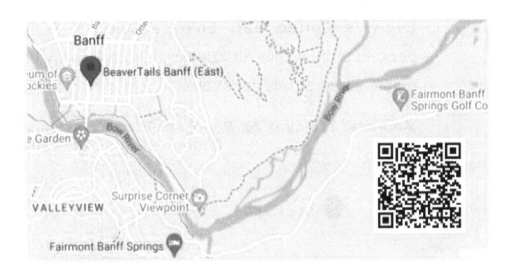

b) **The Candy Store:** This old-fashioned candy shop offers a wide selection of maple candies, fudge, and other treats.

> *Address: 215 Banff Ave, Banff, AB T1L 1A8, Canada*
> *Phone: +1 403-762-3551*

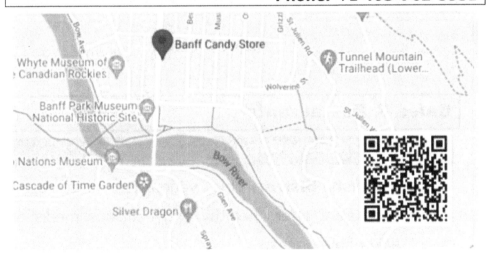

c) **Evelyn's Coffee Bar:** Enjoy a stack of fluffy pancakes or waffles drizzled with locally sourced maple syrup at this cozy café.

> *Address: 218 Lynx St, Banff, AB T1L 1K1, Canada*
> *Phone: +1 403-760-0101*

Cafés & Restaurants

• Budget-Friendly Options:

1. **Nourish Bistro:** This vegetarian and vegan restaurant offers healthy and delicious meals at affordable prices.

Address: 211 Bear St, Banff, AB T1L 1A3, Canada
Phone: +1 403-760-3830

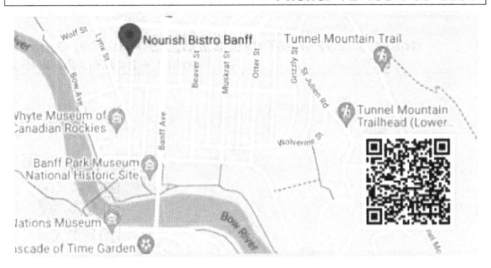

2. **Magpie & Stump:** This lively Mexican restaurant is a great spot for casual dining and margaritas.

Address: 203 Caribou St, Banff, AB T1L 1A3, Canada
Phone: +1 403-762-4454

3. **Eddie Burger + Bar:** Enjoy juicy burgers, crispy fries, and milkshakes at this family-friendly eatery.

> *Address: 137 Banff Ave, Banff, AB T1L 1A4, Canada*
> *Phone: +1 403-762-2491*

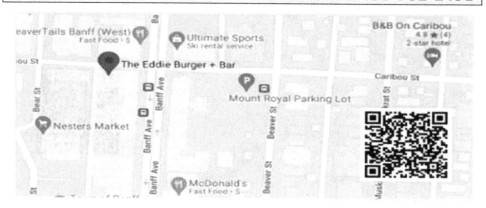

• Mid-Range Dining:

1. **The Maple Leaf:** This restaurant features a menu of Canadian comfort food with a focus on local ingredients.

> *Address: 137 Banff Ave, Banff, AB T1L 1A4, Canada*
> *Phone: +1 403-762-4422*

2. **Park Distillery Restaurant + Bar:** Sample handcrafted spirits and enjoy delicious dishes made with locally sourced ingredients at this distillery-restaurant.

> *Address: 215 Banff Ave, Banff, AB T1L 1A8, Canada*
> *Phone: +1 403-762-5114*

3. **Grizzly House:** Experience a unique fondue dining experience in a rustic setting.

> *Address: 207 Banff Ave, Banff, AB T1L 1A7, Canada*
> *Phone: +1 403-762-4055*

1. **Eden at the Rimrock Resort Hotel:** This award-winning restaurant offers a sophisticated fine dining experience with stunning mountain views.

> *Address: 300 Mountain Ave, Banff, AB T1L 1J2, Canada*
> *Phone: +1 403-762-3356*

2. **The Vermillion Room:** Located in the Fairmont Banff Springs Hotel, this elegant restaurant serves refined Canadian cuisine in a historic setting.

> *Address: 405 Spray Ave, Banff, AB T1L 1J4, Canada*
> *Phone: +1 403-762-2211, +1403-762-6860*

1. **Sky Bistro:** Located at the top of the Banff Gondola, this restaurant offers breathtaking panoramic views while you dine.

Address: 100 Mountain Ave, Banff, AB T1L 1J4, Canada
Phone: +1 403-762-7475, +1403-762-7486

2. **The Juniper Bistro:** Enjoy delicious meals and cocktails on the patio of this bistro, overlooking the stunning Cascade Mountain.

Address: 1 Juniper Way, Banff, AB T1L 1J4, Canada
Phone: +1 403-762-2281,+140-763-6219

Grocery Stores & Markets

- **Banff Townsite:** You'll find several grocery stores in Banff Townsite, including Nester's Market and IGA, where you can stock up on essentials for picnics or self-catering.

- **Banff Farmers' Market:** During the summer months, the Banff Farmers' Market is a great place to find fresh local produce, artisanal goods, and handmade crafts.

With its diverse dining options and abundance of fresh local ingredients, Banff is a culinary destination in its own right. So venture out, explore the flavors, and create your own delicious memories!

CHAPTER 8: BANFF AFTER DARK

When the sun dips below the mountains and paints the sky with hues of orange and purple, Banff's nightlife scene awakens, offering a mix of lively pubs, cultural events, and the awe-inspiring beauty of the night sky.

Bars & Pubs

- **Banff Ave Brewing Co.:** Located on Banff Avenue, this bustling brewpub is a local favorite, offering a wide selection of handcrafted beers, delicious pub fare, and a lively atmosphere. Grab a seat on the patio, enjoy live music, and mingle with fellow travelers and locals alike.

- **The Elk & Oarsman:** This cozy pub is the perfect spot to unwind after a day of adventure. Sink into a comfy armchair by the fireplace, sip on a craft cocktail or local beer, and enjoy the sounds of live music filling the air.

- **Rose & Crown:** Head to the rooftop patio at the Rose & Crown for stunning views of Banff Avenue and Cascade Mountain. This lively bar is known for its fun atmosphere, great  drinks, and delicious pub grub. It's a perfect spot to people-watch and soak up the mountain town vibe.

- **Wild Bill's Legendary Saloon:** Step into the Wild West at this iconic Banff institution. With its rustic décor, live country music, and lively dance floor, Wild Bill's offers a fun and energetic night out. Don't miss their famous mechanical bull – if you dare!

Live Music & Entertainment

- **The Banff Centre for Arts and Creativity:** This world-renowned arts center is a cultural hub, hosting a variety of performances throughout the year. Catch a concert, theater production, or dance performance in one of their state-of-the-art venues.

- **Banff Summer Arts Festival:** If you're visiting during the summer, don't miss the Banff Summer Arts Festival. This vibrant event features outdoor concerts, theater performances, and visual arts exhibitions, showcasing local and international talent.

- **Local Pubs & Bars:** Many of Banff's pubs and bars offer live music on certain nights. Check local listings or ask your hotel concierge for recommendations on where to catch some tunes.

Stargazing & Northern Lights

- **Dark Sky Preserve:** Banff National Park is a designated Dark Sky Preserve, meaning it has exceptional nighttime environments for stargazing. On a clear night, you'll be treated to a dazzling display of stars, planets, and constellations.

- **Best Viewing Spots:** Escape the town lights and head to areas like Lake Minnewanka, Vermilion Lakes, or the Banff Gondola summit for optimal stargazing. Bring a blanket, lie back, and marvel at the celestial wonders above.

- **Northern Lights:** If you're lucky, you might even witness the mesmerizing dance of the Aurora Borealis

(Northern Lights) during the winter months. For the best chance of seeing them, head away from town lights and look to the northern sky on a clear, cold night.

Whether you're seeking a lively night out or a peaceful evening under the stars, Banff has something to offer after dark. So, raise a glass, enjoy the music, and let the magic of Banff's nightlife enchant you.

CHAPTER 9: DAY TRIPS & EXCURSIONS

While Banff National Park offers endless wonders to explore, consider venturing beyond its boundaries for even more unforgettable experiences. These day trips showcase the diverse beauty and attractions of the surrounding areas.

Yoho National Park

Just a short drive west of Banff lies Yoho National Park, a breathtaking wilderness of towering peaks, cascading waterfalls, and emerald-hued lakes.

- **Scenic Highlights:**

  - ➢ Emerald Lake: This jewel-toned lake, surrounded by snow-capped mountains, is a sight to behold. Rent a canoe, hike the lakeshore trail, or simply relax and soak up the tranquility.

  - ➢ Takakkaw Falls: Prepare to be awestruck by one of Canada's highest waterfalls, plunging 384 meters (1,260 feet) into a rocky gorge.

  - ➢ Natural Bridge: Witness the power of water as the Kicking Horse River has carved a natural bridge through solid rock over centuries.

- **Activities:**

  - ➢ Hiking: Explore a network of trails, from easy walks to challenging climbs, offering breathtaking views of the surrounding peaks and valleys.

  - ➢ Scenic Drives: Take a leisurely drive along the Yoho Valley Road, which winds its way through the heart of the park, showcasing its stunning scenery.

  - ➢ Camping: Spend a night under the stars at one of Yoho's scenic campgrounds, immersing yourself in the wilderness.

- **Getting There:**

  - ➢ Yoho National Park is located about a 30-minute drive west of Banff Townsite along the Trans-Canada Highway.

Lake Louise Ski Resort

In winter, Lake Louise Ski Resort transforms into a snowy paradise, offering world-class skiing and snowboarding on its vast slopes. But even in the summer, the resort is a worthy destination, offering a range of activities amidst breathtaking scenery.

- **Winter Activities:**

74

- Skiing & Snowboarding: Carve your way down pristine slopes, from gentle beginner runs to challenging expert terrain.

- Snowshoeing & Cross-Country Skiing: Explore the winter wonderland on snowshoes or cross-country skis, enjoying the crisp mountain air and scenic trails.

- **Summer Activities:**

  - Hiking: Take the Lake Louise Gondola to the top of the mountain and access a network of hiking trails with stunning views.

  - Sightseeing: Admire the beauty of Lake Louise and the surrounding mountains from various viewpoints.

  - Gondola Rides: Enjoy a scenic gondola ride for panoramic vistas of the area, even if you're not skiing or hiking.

- **Getting There:**

  - Lake Louise Ski Resort is located about a 45-minute drive northwest of Banff Townsite along the Trans-Canada Highway. Shuttle buses also operate between Banff and the resort.

Canmore & Kananaskis Country

Just a short drive from Banff, Canmore offers a charming mountain town experience with a vibrant arts and culture scene. Kananaskis Country, a vast wilderness area adjacent to Banff, provides even more opportunities for outdoor adventure.

- **Canmore:**

  - ➤ Explore the town's art galleries, boutiques, and restaurants.

  - ➤ Enjoy the scenic views of the Three Sisters mountain peaks.

  - ➤ Attend a cultural event or festival at the Canmore Nordic Centre.

- **Kananaskis Country:**

  - ➤ Explore the many trails on foot or by bike.

  - ➤ Go camping or rent a cabin in the wilderness.

  - ➤ Enjoy water activities like kayaking or canoeing on the Kananaskis Lakes.

- **Getting There:**

  - ➤ Canmore is located about a 20-minute drive southeast of Banff Townsite.

76

➤ Kananaskis Country is easily accessible from Canmore, with various access points depending on your desired activity.

These day trips offer a taste of the diverse landscapes and experiences that await beyond Banff's borders. So, venture out, explore, and create your own unforgettable adventures in the Canadian Rockies!

CHAPTER 10: ACCOMMODATIONS

Finding the perfect place to rest your head after a day of exploring Banff's wonders is essential. Whether you're seeking budget-friendly options or luxurious retreats, the park offers a variety of accommodations to suit your needs.

Range of Options (Budget to Luxury)

Hostels

1. **HI Banff Alpine Centre:** A social hub for budget travelers, offering dorms, private rooms, and even cabins. Enjoy the lively atmosphere, communal kitchen, and convenient location near downtown Banff.

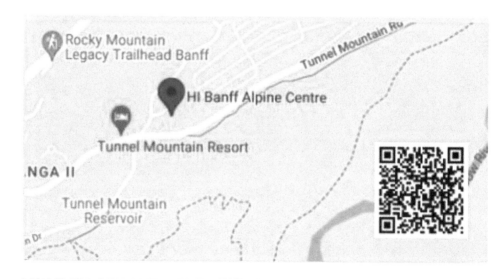

Address: 801 Hidden Ridge Way, Banff, AB T1L 1B3, Canada
Phone: +1 403-762-4123
Price Range: $30-60 USD per night
Facilities: Dorms, private rooms, cabins, communal kitchen, common areas, free Wi-Fi, laundry facilities, bike rentals, on-site restaurant and bar

2. **Samesun Banff:** Another great option for budget-conscious travelers, Samesun Banff offers comfortable dorms and private rooms, a lively bar, and a central location.

Address: 433 Banff Ave, Banff, AB T1L 1B4, Canada
Phone: +1 403-762-4499.
Price Range: $25-50 USD per night
Facilities: Dorms, private rooms, free Wi-Fi, free breakfast, communal kitchen, bar, games room

Campgrounds

3. **Tunnel Mountain Village II Campground:** Nestled amongst the trees with stunning views, this campground offers a range of options from tent sites to fully-equipped cabins. It's perfect for those seeking a classic camping experience close to town.

Address: Tunnel Mountain Rd, Banff, AB T1L 1J5, Canada

Phone: +1 403-762-1550
Price Range: $27-120 USD per night depending on site type and season
Facilities: Tent and RV sites, oTENTiks (equipped campsites), cabins, washrooms, showers, laundry facilities, playground

- **Two Jack Lakeside Campground:** Enjoy lakeside views and easy access to hiking trails at this popular campground. Sites fill up quickly, so be sure to book in advance, especially during peak season.

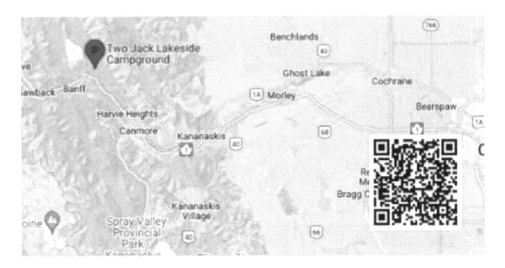

Address: Lake Minnewanka Scenic Dr, Improvement District No. 9, AB T1L 1J5, Canada
Phone: +1 403-762-1550, +1877-737-3783
Price Range: $27-38 USD per night depending on site type and season

Facilities: Tent and RV sites, washrooms, showers, picnic tables, fire pits

Hotels

4. **Banff Ptarmigan Inn:** This cozy hotel offers comfortable rooms, some with mountain views, and a convenient location near downtown Banff.

Address: 345 Banff Ave, Banff, AB T1L 1C2, Canada

Phone: +1 403-762-2233, +1800-661-8310

Price Range: $150-250 USD per night

Facilities: Indoor pool, hot tubs, sauna, steam room, fitness center, on-site restaurant

5. **Moose Hotel & Suites:** This modern hotel features stylish rooms and suites, a rooftop hot pool with mountain views, and a central location on Banff Avenue.

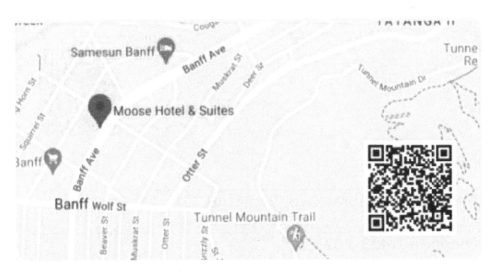

Address: 345 Banff Ave, Banff, AB T1L 1C2, Canada
Phone: +1 403-762-3323
Price Range: $200-400 USD per night
Facilities: Rooftop hot pools, spa, fitness center, on-site restaurants, bar, complimentary breakfast

- **Fairmont Banff Springs:** This iconic castle-like hotel offers a luxurious experience with elegant rooms, multiple dining options, a spa, and a golf course.

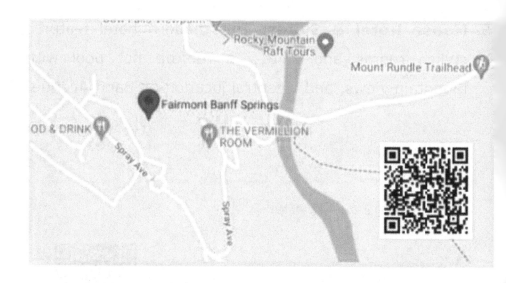

Address: 405 Spray Ave, Banff, AB T1L 1J4, Canada
Phone: +1 403-762-2211
Price Range: $400+ USD per night
Facilities: Multiple restaurants and bars, spa, fitness center, indoor and outdoor pools, golf course, tennis courts, bowling alley, shops

B. Vacation Rentals:

1. **Airbnb & Vrbo:** For a more home-like experience, consider renting a cabin, condo, or chalet through

platforms like Airbnb or Vrbo. You'll find a wide variety of options to suit different group sizes and budgets.

Price Range: Varies depending on the property, size, and location.
Facilities: Amenities vary depending on the property, but often include full kitchens, living areas, and outdoor spaces.

2. **Banff Lodging Co.:** This local company offers a curated selection of vacation rentals in Banff and the surrounding area, including condos, townhomes, and private homes. Their properties are known for their high quality and convenient locations.

Price Range: Varies depending on the property, size, and location.
Facilities: Amenities vary depending on the property, but often include full kitchens, living areas, fireplaces, hot tubs, and stunning mountain views.

Please note that prices and availability for vacation rentals can fluctuate depending on the season and demand. It's always best to book your accommodation well in advance, especially during peak travel times.

CHAPTER 11:
ACTIVITIES & EXPERIENCES

Banff National Park is a haven for outdoor enthusiasts, offering a plethora of activities to immerse yourself in the natural beauty of the Canadian Rockies.

Summer Adventures:

- **Hiking:** Banff's trails cater to all levels, from leisurely strolls to challenging summits.

  ➢ **Easy:**

  - Johnston Canyon: Explore this accessible canyon with its stunning waterfalls and unique rock formations.

  - Tunnel Mountain: Hike to the summit for panoramic views of Banff Townsite and the Bow Valley.

  - Fenland Trail: This gentle loop offers a glimpse into Banff's diverse ecosystems and opportunities for wildlife viewing.

  ➢ **Moderate:**

  - Lake Agnes Trail: Hike to the charming Lake Agnes Tea House, perched high above Lake Louise, and enjoy breathtaking views and a well-deserved cup of tea.

  - Sulphur Mountain (without the gondola): Challenge yourself with a steep but rewarding hike to the summit of Sulphur Mountain, where you'll be rewarded with panoramic vistas.

➢ **Challenging:**

- Plain of the Six Glaciers Trail: This iconic hike leads to a historic tea house nestled amidst glaciers and towering peaks.

- Larch Valley & Sentinel Pass: Experience the golden hues of larch trees in the fall on this scenic hike.

- Devil's Thumb: This challenging scramble offers breathtaking views from the summit but requires experience and proper equipment.

- **Biking:** Pedal your way through Banff's stunning landscapes on a variety of scenic bike routes.

➢ **Banff Legacy Trail:** This paved pathway connects Banff to Canmore, offering a leisurely ride with beautiful views.

➢ **Bow Valley Parkway:** Enjoy a scenic ride along this quieter road, keeping an eye out for wildlife.

➢ **Tunnel Mountain Road:** This challenging climb rewards you with panoramic vistas from the summit.

- **Kayaking & Canoeing:** Glide across Banff's tranquil lakes and rivers, surrounded by majestic mountains.

  - ➢ **Lake Louise & Moraine Lake:** Rent a canoe or kayak and enjoy a peaceful paddle on these iconic lakes.

  - ➢ **Bow River:** Experience the gentle current of the Bow River on a guided or self-guided tour.

  - ➢ **Vermilion Lakes:** These calm lakes offer a serene setting for paddling and birdwatching.

- **Wildlife Viewing:** Banff is teeming with wildlife, so keep your eyes peeled and your camera ready!

  - ➢ **Best Times:** Early morning and dusk are prime times for wildlife spotting.

  - ➢ **Where to Look:** Keep an eye out along the Bow Valley Parkway, the Icefields Parkway, and around lakes and meadows.

  - ➢ **Safety First:** Always maintain a safe distance from wildlife, never feed them, and be aware of your surroundings. Carry bear spray and know how to use it if you're venturing into bear country.

Remember to respect the environment and wildlife, and always prioritize safety when enjoying Banff's outdoor playground.

Winter Activities

When winter blankets Banff in a pristine coat of snow, the park transforms into a magical playground for winter enthusiasts.

Skiing & Snowboarding:

- **Lake Louise Ski Resort:** Carve your way down some of the most scenic slopes in the world, with breathtaking views of Lake Louise and the surrounding peaks. This world-class resort offers terrain for all levels, from gentle beginner runs to challenging expert bowls.

- **Sunshine Village:** Bask in the sunshine and enjoy long, cruisy runs at this high-altitude resort. Sunshine Village boasts diverse terrain, including wide-open bowls, glades, and mogul fields.

- **Mt. Norquay:** This local favorite is known for its challenging terrain and its proximity to Banff Townsite. It's a great option for experienced skiers and snowboarders looking for a thrill.

Snowshoeing:

Strap on a pair of snowshoes and explore Banff's winter wonderland at your own pace.

- **Johnston Canyon:** The snow-covered canyon and frozen waterfalls create a magical winter scene Anyone can enjoy this well-kept trail.

- **Sundance Canyon:** Experience the tranquility of this lesser-known canyon in the winter, where snow-covered trees and frozen waterfalls create a picture-perfect setting.

Ice Skating:

Glide across the ice with the majestic mountains as your backdrop.

- **Lake Louise:** Skate on the iconic Lake Louise, surrounded by stunning scenery. Check for rink conditions and availability, as the lake may not always be frozen solid enough for skating.

- **Banff Recreation Grounds:** This outdoor rink offers a fun and family-friendly atmosphere, with skate rentals available.

Dog Sledding:

Experience the thrill of gliding through the snow-covered forests behind a team of energetic huskies. Several outfitters in Banff offer dog sledding tours, ranging from short introductory rides to multi-day adventures.

Relaxation & Wellness

- **Banff Upper Hot Springs:** Soak away your cares in the soothing waters of these natural hot springs, surrounded by breathtaking mountain views. It's the perfect way to unwind after a day of winter activities.

- **Spas:** Treat yourself to a relaxing massage, facial, or other pampering treatment at one of Banff's many spas. Many hotels offer on-site spas, while others are located in town or at nearby resorts.

- **Yoga & Meditation:** Find your inner peace with a yoga or meditation class. Several studios in Banff offer classes for all levels, or you can practice outdoors in a scenic location.

Festivals & Events

- **Banff Mountain Film and Book Festival:** This world-renowned festival celebrates mountain culture and adventure through inspiring films, captivating books, and engaging presentations.

- **Christmas in Banff:** Experience the festive spirit with holiday lights, caroling, and special events throughout the town.

Banff's winter charm extends beyond its snowy slopes and frozen lakes. Embrace the cozy atmosphere, engage in seasonal treats, and create unforgettable memories in this winter wonderland.

CHAPTER 12: PRACTICAL TIPS

Navigating Banff National Park requires more than just knowing where to go and what to see; it's also about understanding and respecting the local customs, the delicate ecosystem, and the wildlife that call this place home.

Local Customs & Etiquette

- **Tipping:** Tipping is customary in Banff for good service. In restaurants and bars, a 15-20% tip is expected. For taxis, round up the fare or add a few dollars. Tour guides and other service providers also appreciate tips for their expertise and assistance.

- **Respect for Nature:** Banff's pristine environment is its greatest treasure. Help preserve its beauty by practicing Leave No Trace principles. Take your trash with you, stick to the trails, and leave the plants and animals alone.

- **Outdoor Ethics:**

  ➢ When hiking or camping, be mindful of your impact on the environment. Stay on marked trails, avoid shortcuts, and pack out all waste.

  ➢ Respect wildlife by observing from a safe distance and never approaching or feeding animals. Keep in mind, you're a guest in their home.

  ➢ Be prepared for changing weather conditions by dressing in layers and carrying essential gear like rain gear and a first-aid kit.

  ➢ Always let someone know your hiking or camping plans, including your expected return time.

Things to Avoid

- **Feeding Wildlife:** Feeding wildlife, even seemingly harmless creatures like squirrels or birds, can disrupt their natural behavior and create dangerous situations for both humans and animals. Admire wildlife from afar and let them forage for their own food.

- **Crowded Areas:** Popular attractions like Lake Louise and Moraine Lake can get very busy, especially during peak season. Consider visiting early in the morning or later in the evening to avoid the crowds and enjoy a more peaceful experience. Alternatively, explore some of Banff's lesser-known trails and viewpoints for a more secluded adventure.

- **Unpreparedness:** Banff's mountain environment can be unpredictable. Before heading out for any outdoor activity, check the weather forecast, pack appropriate clothing and gear, and let someone know where you're going and when you expect to be back.

- **Ignoring Trail Closures and Warnings:** For your safety, pay attention to trail closures and warnings posted by Parks Canada. These closures are often in place due to wildlife activity, trail maintenance, or hazardous conditions. Respect these closures and choose alternative trails to ensure a safe and enjoyable experience.

- **Leaving Valuables in Your Car:** Unfortunately, car break-ins can occur, especially in popular tourist areas. Avoid leaving valuables in your car, and if you must, keep them out of sight and lock your vehicle securely.

- **Hiking Alone in Remote Areas:** While Banff's trails are generally safe, it's always best to hike with a partner, especially in more remote or challenging areas. Before you head out, tell someone where you're hiking and when you plan to return. It's important for your safety.

- **Underestimating Altitude Sickness:** If you're not accustomed to higher altitudes, be mindful of the potential for altitude sickness. Chill out, stay hydrated, and listen to what your body's telling you. If you experience symptoms like headache, nausea, or shortness of breath, descend to a lower altitude.

- **Forgetting Your Camera:** Banff's scenery is truly breathtaking, so don't miss the opportunity to capture those memories! Bring a camera or smartphone to document your adventures and share your experiences with friends and family.

- **Overpacking:** While it's important to be prepared, avoid overpacking. Remember that laundry facilities are available in Banff Townsite and many hotels. Pack light and prioritize versatile clothing that can be layered for different weather conditions.

- **Not Booking Activities in Advance:** Popular activities like gondola rides, boat cruises, and wildlife tours can sell out quickly, especially during peak season. Book your activities in advance to avoid disappointment.

- **Missing the Sunrise or Sunset:** Banff's skies are truly magical at dawn and dusk. Set your alarm early or stay out late to witness the breathtaking colors and experience the park's tranquility.

By following these practical tips and being a responsible visitor, you'll help preserve Banff's natural beauty for generations to come while enjoying a safe and fulfilling experience in this breathtaking national park.

Staying Safe & Connected: Emergency Contacts and Communication Tips

Banff National Park prioritizes visitor safety, but it's always wise to be prepared and informed, especially in a wilderness setting.

Emergency Numbers:

- **911:** In any emergency, dial 911 for police, ambulance, or fire services. This number is free to call from any phone, including public payphones.

- **Parks Canada Emergency Dispatch:** 1-888-762-1422, 403-762-1470 (For emergencies within Banff National Park)

Cell Phone Coverage:

While cell phone coverage is generally good in Banff Townsite and along major highways, it can be spotty or non-existent in more remote areas of the park. Keep this in mind when venturing off the beaten path, and consider carrying a satellite communication device or informing someone of your itinerary if you're hiking or camping in remote areas.

Visitor Centers:

The Banff Visitor Centre is an excellent resource for maps, brochures, trail information, and safety tips. Park staff can answer your questions, provide updates on trail conditions,

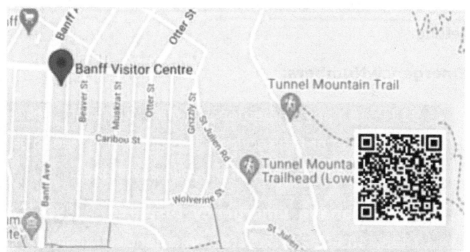

and offer guidance on wildlife safety and responsible recreation practices. Be sure to stop by before heading out on any adventures!

Languages Spoken:

- **English:** English is the primary language spoken in Banff and throughout the Canadian Rockies. You'll have no trouble communicating with locals, park staff, and fellow travelers.

- **French:** While French is one of Canada's official languages, it's less commonly spoken in Banff.

However, you might encounter some bilingual signage or services.

By being prepared and informed, you can ensure a safe and enjoyable experience in Banff National Park. Remember, prioritize safety, respect the environment, and embrace the spirit of adventure!

Medical Services & Pharmacies

While we hope you stay healthy during your Banff adventure, it's essential to be prepared for any unforeseen medical needs.

- **Banff Mineral Springs Hospital:** This is the main hospital in Banff, providing 24-hour emergency care and a range of medical services.

Address: 303 Lynx St, Banff, AB T1L 1G8, Canada

Phone: +1 403-762-2222

- **Banff Medical Clinic:** This clinic offers walk-in and appointment-based medical services for non-emergency situations.

Address: 315 Marten St, Banff, AB T1L 1B3, Canada

Phone: +1 403-762-4444

- **Pharmacies:**

101

- ➢ **Banff Pharmacy:** Conveniently located in downtown Banff, this pharmacy offers prescription medications, over-the-counter drugs, and health supplies.

- ➢ **Shoppers Drug Mart:** Another pharmacy option in Banff Townsite, providing a wide selection of medications and health products.

Tips:

- **Travel Insurance:** Ensure you have comprehensive travel insurance that covers medical expenses in case of illness or injury.

- **Medications:** Pack any necessary prescription medications and a basic first-aid kit for minor injuries.

- **Altitude Sickness:** Be aware of the symptoms of altitude sickness, which can occur at higher elevations. If you experience headache, nausea, or shortness of breath, seek medical attention.

By being prepared and knowing where to find medical assistance, you can ensure a safe and healthy trip to Banff National Park.

CHAPTER 13: SUGGESTED ITINERARIES

Whether you have a few days or a week to explore, here are a few sample itineraries to inspire your Banff adventure. Remember, these are just suggestions - feel free to mix and match activities based on your interests and the time you have available.

Short & Sweet (2-3 Days)

Day 1:

- **Morning**: Explore the charming town of Banff. Stroll down Banff Avenue, browse the shops and galleries, and grab a coffee at a local café.

- **Afternoon**: Take a thrilling ride up Sulphur Mountain on the Banff Gondola. Enjoy panoramic views from the summit, explore the interpretive center, and take a walk along the boardwalk.

- **Evening**: Enjoy a delicious dinner at a restaurant with mountain views, followed by a leisurely stroll along the Bow River.

Day 2:

- **Morning**: Begin a scenic drive to Lake Louise and Moraine Lake. Marvel at the turquoise waters and surrounding peaks.

- **Afternoon**: Choose your adventure! Hike to the Lake Agnes Tea House for breathtaking views and a rewarding cup of tea, rent a canoe and paddle on Lake Louise, or simply relax on the lakeshore and soak up the scenery.

- **Evening**: Head back to Banff and enjoy a delicious meal at a local restaurant.

Day 3 (Optional)

- If you have an extra day, consider driving the scenic Bow Valley Parkway, stopping at Johnston Canyon for a hike and enjoying the waterfalls.

- Alternatively, take a wildlife viewing tour for a chance to spot elk, deer, bighorn sheep, and other animals in their natural habitat.

This short itinerary offers a taste of Banff's highlights, perfect for a weekend getaway or a quick trip to the mountains.

A Week in Banff

For those with more time to explore, a week in Banff allows for a deeper dive into the park's natural wonders and a wider range of experiences.

Days 1-3:

- Follow the Short & Sweet itinerary to get acquainted with Banff Townsite, Lake Louise, Moraine Lake, and the Banff Gondola. These iconic landmarks and activities provide a solid foundation for your Banff adventure.

Day 4:

- Take a breathtaking drive on the Icefields Parkway, renowned for its stunning scenery. This 232-kilometer (144-mile) highway winds through the heart of the Canadian Rockies, offering breathtaking views of glaciers, waterfalls, and turquoise lakes. Make stops at iconic spots like Peyto Lake, Bow Lake, and the Columbia Icefield for photos and short hikes.

Day 5:

- Venture into Yoho National Park, just a short drive from Banff. Hike to the stunning Emerald Lake or marvel at the power of Takakkaw Falls, one of

Canada's highest waterfalls. Explore the park's scenic trails, enjoy a picnic lunch, and immerse yourself in the tranquility of this pristine wilderness.

Day 6:

- Choose a unique activity that speaks to your sense of adventure. Saddle up for a horseback riding excursion through scenic meadows and forests, experience the thrill of whitewater rafting on the Bow River, or soar above the mountains on a scenic helicopter tour for breathtaking aerial views.

Day 7:

- After a few days of exploration, take some time to relax and recharge. Soak in the warm waters of the Banff Upper Hot Springs, surrounded by stunning mountain scenery. Or, pamper yourself with a massage or other rejuvenating treatment at one of Banff's luxurious spas.

Extended Stay (10+ days)

If you're fortunate enough to have an extended stay in Banff, the possibilities are endless.

- Combine the above itineraries and add additional activities that pique your interest.

- Consider exploring further afield with day trips to Jasper National Park, known for its wildlife and rugged beauty, or the charming mountain town of Canmore.

- Take advantage of Banff's diverse outdoor activities. In summer, hike to stunning summits, bike along scenic trails, or go canoeing or kayaking on pristine lakes. In winter, hit the slopes for world-class skiing and snowboarding, explore snow-covered trails on snowshoes, or go ice skating under a starry sky.

No matter how long you stay, Banff National Park will leave a lasting impression on your heart and soul. With its stunning scenery, abundant wildlife, and endless opportunities for adventure, it's a destination that will keep calling you back for years to come.

CONCLUSION

As you close this pocket guide, we hope you're filled with excitement and anticipation for the unforgettable journey that lies ahead. Banff National Park, with its majestic mountains, pristine lakes, and abundant wildlife, is a destination that promises to awaken your senses and leave you in awe of nature's grandeur.

Whether you're seeking thrilling outdoor adventures, peaceful moments of solitude, or simply a chance to reconnect with the natural world, Banff has something to offer everyone. From iconic landmarks like Lake Louise and Moraine Lake to hidden gems like the Ink Pots and Sundance Canyon, every corner of the park holds a unique treasure waiting to be discovered.

As you commence your Banff adventure, remember to:

- **Embrace the Spirit of Adventure:** Step outside your comfort zone, try new activities, and explore the park's diverse landscapes.

- **Respect the Environment and Wildlife:** Practice Leave No Trace principles, observe wildlife from a safe distance, and be a responsible steward of this precious ecosystem.

- **Create Lasting Memories:** Capture the beauty of Banff through photos, journal entries, and shared experiences with loved ones.

This pocket guide has provided you with the essential tools to navigate Banff with confidence, but the true magic lies in the journey itself.

So, pack your bags, lace up your hiking boots, and get ready to experience the wonders of Banff National Park. We can't wait to hear about your adventures!

SAFE TRAVELS AND HAPPY EXPLORING!

Word Search Fun

Take a break from exploring and challenge yourself with these word searches! They're a fun way to test your knowledge of the city's landmarks, neighborhoods, cuisine, and more. So, grab a pen and see how many words you can find!

HOW TO PLAY

- **Find the words:** Carefully scan the grid and try to spot the hidden words.

- **Any direction goes:** The words can be horizontal, vertical, diagonal, or even backwards!

- **Sharing is caring:** Words can share letters as they cross over each other, so keep your eyes peeled!

- **Circle or highlight:** Once you find a word, circle it or highlight it with a pen or pencil.

- **Check them off:** Use the word list (below each page) to keep track of the words you've found below.

- **No peeking!** Try to find them all on your own first. If you need help, scan the QR code below to access the solutions.

LANDMARKS

```
O  L  L  N  M  C  D  E  Q  G  E  U  C  A  E
M  F  A  J  A  U  D  K  J  R  U  O  A  Q  C
Y  J  T  V  R  R  E  F  D  O  M  E  S  M  A
S  M  E  E  E  E  H  S  F  X  Q  V  T  U  L
T  R  E  T  S  Z  S  A  U  I  Z  E  L  E  A
N  S  A  B  X  T  Z  Y  O  M  L  O  E  S  P
T  R  O  F  D  A  A  T  E  V  N  C  H  S  X
C  P  R  B  L  C  T  T  S  G  Y  M  L  O  S
W  W  E  P  Y  O  A  S  E  T  C  Q  G  L  G
X  L  I  H  R  Y  I  N  K  H  A  R  B  O  R
T  W  C  G  Z  C  F  S  A  G  V  T  T  C  M
Z  R  A  F  O  O  E  F  L  L  K  O  U  I  T
A  M  L  D  R  G  P  J  H  A  W  N  N  E  E
R  J  G  E  U  Q  S  O  M  E  N  A  M  C  M
P  Q  S  P  I  R  E  R  R  A  R  D  X  Z  P
P  T  E  O  E  W  B  D  C  E  U  U  P  M  L
U  O  N  A  C  L  O  V  T  R  I  K  A  E
H  B  R  I  D  G  E  H  C  R  U  H  C  N  P
M  W  G  J  Z  J  D  Z  N  F  U  J  X  O  X
L  K  A  J  C  N  H  L  P  F  V  U  C  R  H
```

Arch -Bridge -Canal -Castle -Cavern -Church -Cliff- Colosseum
Crater -Dome- Estate- Fjord-Forest -Fort -Geyser -Glacier-
Grotto- Harbor -Island- Manor- Minaret -Mosque -Museum-
Palace -Plaza -Spire- Statue -Temple -Tower- Volcano

WILDLIFE

```
A  R  U  F  O  V  H  V  D  E  A  X  D  T  N
F  I  S  H  P  E  R  A  E  T  L  O  K  G  O
Y  I  R  A  E  B  K  J  E  M  V  G  O  J  R
K  C  U  D  Y  N  L  F  R  Q  L  A  A  R  E
K  V  N  N  Q  M  E  M  O  X  T  Z  P  E  H
L  W  W  E  S  O  O  G  N  X  O  S  C  P  B
I  A  A  B  W  Q  C  Y  R  C  A  L  F  U  D
F  A  E  H  O  T  L  Q  A  Y  C  G  C  O  B
R  K  J  S  Z  J  M  O  O  S  E  P  V  R  T
C  W  W  U  X  O  U  E  B  L  F  E  G  N  N
O  X  O  R  R  W  G  U  K  F  S  Z  C  S  A
B  K  J  P  E  L  Z  O  X  R  M  A  S  E  W
L  Q  U  K  K  N  B  L  H  R  X  G  X  O  S
S  P  Z  C  Q  R  F  I  T  O  L  I  T  F  V
G  V  U  U  D  R  R  U  Y  C  K  J  X  A  H
A  B  Y  V  O  A  O  H  D  S  S  U  B  V  A
A  D  I  O  S  R  G  E  M  M  A  R  G  F  C
T  Y  R  U  T  U  B  W  W  X  W  R  P  F  T
K  B  K  I  W  O  L  F  D  U  Z  T  E  T  S
S  O  A  V  B  C  W  H  U  U  B  C  N  K  Z
```

Bear- Bird- Boar -Buck -Calf- Cub- Deer- Dove- Duck -Eagle
Elk -Fawn -Fish- Fox -Frog- Goat -Goose- Hawk- Heron -Lynx
Moose -Newt -Owl -Pup- Ram- Seal- Swan -Trout -Wolf- Wren

112

```
H  J  A  J  T  T  C  M  N  Q  A  T  M  B  V
Z  Z  B  R  S  A  G  X  U  V  J  N  A  A  G
F  V  A  E  N  G  O  R  G  E  D  E  E  O  Y
S  I  R  Y  K  C  R  Y  O  N  J  C  R  A  M
L  O  O  N  Z  E  H  I  E  V  G  S  T  G  V
F  N  Q  Y  N  T  E  B  D  L  E  E  S  E  G
B  R  C  V  A  S  K  R  P  G  L  D  J  Y  R
T  R  A  P  X  J  E  G  C  T  E  A  W  I  Y
T  I  I  P  E  A  K  V  I  D  Q  N  V  H  O
N  C  R  L  L  X  P  M  B  W  O  D  A  E  M
U  S  N  L  U  L  M  S  F  R  F  X  O  W  R
O  D  S  H  L  U  Y  W  W  J  O  Z  X  L  K
M  Y  O  O  S  C  R  I  J  E  Z  O  E  M  S
W  O  H  P  M  L  I  T  T  U  E  D  K  W  R
S  E  E  R  T  A  V  C  N  O  G  R  T  O  N
Z  M  A  D  X  K  E  H  E  E  I  X  C  Q  T
E  T  U  O  R  E  R  B  C  B  H  K  R  S  K
W  V  G  Y  G  E  P  A  S  Q  S  O  P  E  I
E  W  E  G  S  Q  A  C  A  B  M  I  L  C  U
B  R  I  D  G  E  Z  K  D  E  J  R  T  I  Q
```

Ascent-Bend- Bridge- Brook- Cairn -Canyon- Climb -Creek- Descent Forest- Gorge- Grove- Lake- Ledge- Meadow- Moss- Mount- Path - Peak Ridge -River- Rocks -Route- Scree -Stream- Summit- Switchback Trail -Trees Valley

ACTIVITIES

```
R E P S R F C K H W Q O B I R
C P D E L U F E C S U A K L Y
V I K I D E O R D E I S L K S
B C U Y R A D T P T R F B T C
S N B I E K L L L A L U R A T
M I W S A K A R Z K W O B C B
W C V Y W Y I T O S L C P S B
X A A D D U Q B D L P L M N I
M K L B A K E E V V M Z V O N
L N Y K C N F D W M A Q H W M
K J N Z X Z C B C B C P L S D
O Q H B M V B E A Z A I B H W
A W I E E M A I E C M M D O A
E S L E E P C X S U I O I E T
K O F W D E M O L L J N N N C
I V E R L X M Q C R Q B E U H
H I I C O O K E R O L P X E P
V V P A I N T D A E R T I C B
E A J V P B K M G D H X U E T
U F N Q E A O Y Z V I S I T J
```

Bike-Camp-Climb-Cook-Dance-Dine-Drive-Explore-Fish-Hike
Kayak-Paint-Pedal-Picnic-Play-Read-Ride-Skate-Ski-Sleep
Sled-Snowshoe-Stroll-Swim-Tour-Trek-View-Visit-Walk-Watch

Answers?

Want to check your answers to the word search puzzles? Simply scan the QR code below to access the solutions.

Has this book been helpful to you in any way? If so, we'd be delighted if you could share your experience with other travelers by leaving a review on Amazon.

Your feedback helps us improve and lets others discover the magic of Banff too!

Travel Adventures

_____
_____
_____
_____
_____
_____
_____
_____
_____
_____
_____
_____
_____
_____
_____
_____
_____
_____
_____
_____
_____
_____
_____

Travel Adventures

_____
_____
_____
_____
_____
_____
_____
_____
_____
_____
_____
_____
_____
_____
_____
_____
_____
_____
_____
_____
_____
_____
_____

KNOW BEFORE YOU GO

BANFF

Pocket Travel Guide

Concise but Detailed

John Stone C.

Made in United States
North Haven, CT
06 January 2025

64076646R00065